Planning

A Manual for Reaching Your Objectives Clearly and Specifically

By

Israel Daniel

Disclaimer

By Israel Daniel, copyright © 2024. All rights reserved. This ebook's content is intended solely for informative and educational purposes. It is not meant to serve as a replacement for expert financial guidance. This ebook's publishers and writers are not financial counselors; thus, the information inside should not be interpreted as individual financial advice. Before making any financial decisions or putting any of the methods covered in this ebook into practice, readers are strongly advised to speak with licensed financial advisors. Any harm or injury arising from reliance on the information supplied herein is disclaimed by the writers and publishers.

Table of contents

Introduction
Chapter 1: Overview of Planning: The Key to Success
- How to Define Planning
- The Value of Planning in Everyday Life

Chapter 2: The Process of Planning: From Concept to Implementation
- Determining the Aim and Objective
- Establishing Smart Objectives
- Sample of Smart Objectives

- Finding the Resources That Are Available
- Evaluating Limitations and Resources
- Recognizing Limitations
- Formulating a Plan for Risk Management

- Formulating a Detailed Plan
- Setting Objectives
- Establishing a Schedule and Deciding Who Is Responsible
- Periodic Evaluation and Modification

Chapter 3: Instruments and Methods for Efficient Planning
- Tools for Time Management
- Strategies for Organizations
- Apps for Planning and Technology

Chapter 4: Setting and Achieving Effective Goals: Having Clearly Defined Objectives
- SMART Objectives
- Methods of Prioritization
- Suggestions for Maintaining Focus

Chapter 5: Getting Past Planning Obstacles: Managing Uncertainty with Resilience
- Handling Uncertainty
- Controlling anxiety and stress
- Adaptability and Flexibility

Chapter 6: Case Studies for Effective Planning: Gaining Knowledge from Actual Cases
- Individual Scheduling: A Day in the Life

- Crisis Management Planning: Actual Case Studies

Chapter 7: Planning's Future: Managing Change in a Changing World
- Planning Trends
- How Technology Affects Planning
- Planning's Function in a Changing World

Conclusion and Next Moves: Equipping You for Success in Future Planning
- An overview of the main ideas
- Sources for Additional Education
- Motivation for Ongoing Planning Achievement

Introduction

The goal of "planning" is to provide a thorough understanding of planning for both individuals and businesses by providing useful strategies and insights. It seeks to provide readers with the information and abilities necessary to successfully plan, whether for company ventures or personal objectives. The book is divided into multiple important sections:

The Planning Process: This part covers subjects including goal-setting, resource evaluation, and timeline creation as it dives into the methodical approach to planning.

Tools and Strategies for Planning: This section offers readers a range of tools and approaches, such as technology-driven solutions, organizational strategies, and time management techniques, to help in planning.

Effective Goal Setting: The concepts of goal-setting are examined in this section, with an emphasis on prioritization strategies and SMART goals (specific, measurable, achievable, relevant, and time-bound).

Overcoming Planning Challenges: This section discusses typical planning challenges and provides solutions for handling stress, remaining flexible, and coping with ambiguity.

Case Studies in Effective Planning: Readers will obtain insights into effective planning in both personal and professional contexts, including project management and crisis planning, through the use of real-world examples.

The Future of Planning: This section examines how planning will develop going forward by examining new trends and the effects of technology. Through adherence to the guidelines and methods presented in the book, readers can cultivate practical planning abilities that benefit them in every aspect of their lives.

Chapter 1: Overview of Planning: The Key to Success

A basic idea that affects all parts of our lives is planning. Planning creates the foundation for success, whether it is in terms of personal objectives or career successes. This part delves into the fundamental components of planning, emphasizing its definition, significance, and an outline of the objectives of the book "Planning.".

How to Define Planning

Planning is the process of setting goals, figuring out how to get there, and allocating resources and deadlines to reach those targets. It requires a blend of strategic planning, flexibility, and foresight. Planning is, at its most basic, imagining the future and drawing up a strategy to get there.

Effective decision-making is made possible by a well-crafted plan, which reduces uncertainty and offers direction and clarity. It facilitates risk minimization, effective resource allocation, and priority setting for both people and companies. Planning is a useful instrument for monitoring advancement and guaranteeing responsibility.

Planning can be as easy as making a daily to-do list or as difficult as coming up with a multi-year business plan. Whatever its scope, all successful planning has several things in common: a defined objective, well-defined goals, and a methodical strategy for reaching those goals.

The Value of Planning in Everyday Life

One cannot stress the importance of planning in daily life. It is essential for assisting people in managing their time, obligations, and interpersonal connections. People can establish balance, lessen stress, and make room for their own personal development by preparing.

Having a well-planned daily life has several advantages.

- **Better Time Management:** People who

plan their days make better use of their time and do critical activities without feeling overburdened.
- **Decreased Stress**: People can concentrate on what has to be done rather than worrying about the future when there is a clear strategy in place, as it lessens uncertainty.
- **Enhanced Productivity**: When people have a plan in place, they may work more productively and accomplish their goals. Improved
- **Decision-Making**: By offering a framework for thought-out decision-making, planning lowers the likelihood of rash decisions or pointless diversions.
- **Enhanced Accountability**: By laying out expectations and deadlines in detail, a plan encourages people to be more accountable and fulfill their promises. Apart from the advantages

it offers personally, professional situations necessitate careful planning.

Planning is essential for organizations to meet their strategic goals, distribute resources, and adapt to shifting market conditions. Planning well can increase creativity, profitability, and customer pleasure.

Chapter 2: The Process of Planning: From Concept to Implementation

Planning is the art and science of turning concepts into doable actions. This section of the book "Planning" walks readers through the crucial steps of the planning process, from setting goals to drafting a thorough plan. Let's examine the essential elements of this procedure: determining the aims and objectives, evaluating the available resources and limitations, and formulating a detailed strategy.

Determining the Aims and Objectives

Any effective planning process starts with defining specific goals and objectives. This is identifying your goals and establishing a precise course for your actions. While objectives are the precise steps or actions needed to achieve goals, goals are the overall outcomes.

Establishing smart objectives

Using the SMART framework, which guarantees that goals are Specific, Measurable, Achievable, Relevant, and Time-bound, is an efficient way to develop goals.
Specific: A goal needs to be well-defined and exact. Steer clear of ambiguous language and concentrate on your specific goals.

- **Measurable**: Specify benchmarks for tracking advancement. This helps you stay motivated and track your accomplishments.
- **Achievable:** Considering your existing resources and limitations, goals should be reasonable and doable.
- **Relevant**: Make sure the goal is important to you or your company and fits in with your larger goals.
- **Time-bound**: Establish a deadline to instill a sense of urgency and promote steady advancement.

Samples of Smart Objectives

- Increase sales by 15% over the next 6 months.
- Complete a marathon within 4 hours by the end of the year.
- Launch a new product line by Q3, achieving at least 10% market share.

Evaluating Limitations and Resources

The next stage after establishing your objectives is to assess the resources at your disposal and any potential barriers. This evaluation assists you in determining what is realistic and what modifications might be necessary.

Finding the Resources That Are Available

Time, money, skills, technology, and people are examples of resources. Make a list of all the resources you own and note any gaps that require filling. At this point, it's also important to decide which tasks will be assigned to whom and what tools or equipment will be needed.

Recognizing Limitations

Constraints are things that could prevent or restrict advancement.

These can be external, like market conditions or legal limitations, or internal, like restricted staffing or budgets. In order to prevent surprises later in the process, identify the limits early on. Think about ways to get over these challenges, such as redistributing resources, learning new abilities, or collaborating with outside specialists.

Formulating a Plan for Risk Management

An effective way to handle limitations and possible hazards is by developing a risk management plan. This entails locating possible hazards, evaluating their impact and likelihood, and creating plans to control or lessen them. By being proactive, you may minimize interruptions and maintain the planning process's direction.

Formulating a Detailed Plan

Making a thorough, step-by-step strategy comes last after

objectives have been established and resources have been evaluated. This plan gives you a defined job and milestone sequence to help you stay on track from beginning to end.

Dividing the Scheme into Doable Steps

Although achieving a complex goal may seem overwhelming, it is easier to carry out when broken down into smaller, more manageable steps. Every step ought to have a distinct goal, an accountable party, and a deadline for fulfillment.

Setting Objectives

Milestones are important junctures in the trip that signify noteworthy advancements. They facilitate the tracking of the overall plan's progress and offer occasions for celebration of accomplishments. Milestones also provide an opportunity to modify the plan in light of fresh knowledge or evolving conditions.

Establishing a Schedule and Deciding Who Is Responsible

A schedule indicates when each task needs to be finished, helping to keep the plan on course. Assign tasks to people or groups to maintain responsibility and clarity. This facilitates coordination of activities and fosters a sense of ownership.

Periodic Evaluation and Modification

The planning process is dynamic. It's critical to periodically examine the plan to make sure your goals and objectives are still being met. Modifications can be required in light of developments or outside events. A flexible plan permits modification while maintaining focus on the main objectives. If you adhere to this thorough planning approach, you'll have a well-defined route to reaching your objectives and the resources you need to overcome obstacles and succeed.

Chapter 3: Instruments and Methods for Efficient Planning

Setting objectives and making schedules are only the first steps in planning; successful plan execution also calls for the use of the appropriate tools and processes.
This section of "Planning" covers technology and planning apps, organizational strategies, time management tools, and other tools and techniques that support the planning process.

Tools for Time Management

Effective planning is based on good time management. Making the most of the time at your disposal is essential to achieving your goals. Here are some essential resources to aid with effective time management:

1. Lists of things to do

To-do lists are a straightforward yet effective technique for task organization. They enable you to divide more ambitious objectives into more doable, smaller tasks. You can make lists on a daily, weekly, or monthly basis to make sure you don't forget any important tasks and stay on schedule.

- Digital To-Do Lists: You can access your tasks from anywhere with the help of apps like Todoist, Microsoft To Do, and Google Keep. These to-do lists are digital and can be synchronized across devices.
- Physical To-Do Lists: Some people find that writing down their things on paper is a more physical experience. For individuals who favor this method, planners and bullet notebooks are common options.

2. Blocking Time

Time blocking is breaking up your day into discrete periods for various jobs or pursuits. By using this technique, you can make sure that you give each activity enough time and steer clear of multitasking, which can lower productivity.

- Calendar-Based Time Blocking: You can set aside particular hours for work, meetings, exercise, and other activities by using digital calendars like Google Calendar or Outlook.
- Pomodoro Technique: This method makes use of timed bursts; usually, 25 minutes of concentrated work are interspersed with a brief break. This approach can be implemented with the use of apps like Forest and Focus@Will.

3. Setting task priorities

Setting priorities for your work is crucial to time management success. Task prioritization tools and methods include:

- Eisenhower Matrix: This system divides work into four sections according to its significance and urgency. It assists you in assigning or removing less important chores so that you can concentrate on what really matters.
- ABC Prioritization: This method divides jobs into priority levels (A, B, and C) according to their urgency and significance. It gives you advice on what to do initially.

Strategies for Organizations

Planning that works involves organization. Processes can be streamlined and orderly with the use of organizational strategies.

The following are some typical tactics to think about:

1.1 5S Approach

A strategy for arranging areas that is useful in many contexts, including manufacturing, is called the 5S methodology. Organize, shine, standardize, sustain and sort are its. By implementing this technique, you may decrease clutter and boost productivity at your workspace.

2. Systems for managing documents

Document organization is essential to successful planning. Documents can be safely stored, arranged, and shared with the help of document management systems (DMS), such as Google Drive, Dropbox, and OneDrive. They also offer collaborative tools and version control.

3. Software for Project Management

Project management software can be quite helpful for bigger projects. Asana, Monday.com, and Trello are a few examples of tools that let you make project boards, assign tasks, set deadlines, and monitor progress.

They also make teamwork possible, which improves accountability and communication.

Apps for Planning and Technology

Modern planning heavily relies on technology. The planning process can be streamlined with a variety of apps and software solutions, from task management to goal setting. The following are a few of the most well-liked planning applications and their uses:

1. Evernote

Evernote is a feature-rich note-taking application that lets you take notes, save online material, and arrange data. It is helpful for research, list-making, and brainstorming.

2. Trello

Trello organizes tasks and projects using a card-based approach. It's perfect for visually tracking and planning your progress, letting you transfer activities between different completion phases.

3. Calendar on Google

A strong scheduling tool that works with other Google services is Google Calendar. Planning for both personal and professional purposes is made easy with the ability to organize events, set reminders, and share calendars with others.

4. Thought

Notion is a single workspace that integrates calendars, databases, project management tools, and notes. Because of its great customization capabilities, you can

Chapter 4: Setting and Achieving Effective Goals: Having Clearly Defined Objectives

Setting goals is the first step in achieving success in any undertaking. It gives guidance, inspires action, and aids in tracking advancement. Effective goal-setting strategies are covered in this section of "planning," with an emphasis on SMART objectives, prioritization strategies, and pointers for maintaining focus. To learn how to create attainable goals and keep moving in the right direction toward them, let's go into each subject in more detail.

SMART Objectives

Setting SMART goals is a popular technique for ensuring that objectives are specific and doable. It stands for time-bound, relevant, specific, measurable, achievable, and achievable. Here's a thorough explanation of each element and how to use it to achieve your objectives:

- Specific: Objectives must be precise and unmistakable. Clearly state your goals for yourself. A particular aim might be to "lose 10 pounds by the end of the year through exercise and a healthy diet," as opposed to a

general one like "get in shape."
- Measurable: In order to monitor your progress, your goals need to be measurable. This entails establishing standards or measures for achievement. A measurable goal would be to "complete a 5K run in under 30 minutes," for instance.
- Realistic: Given the constraints and resources at hand, objectives should be reasonable and reachable. Setting unachievable objectives can cause dissatisfaction and despair, even when ambitious aims can be inspirational. Think about whether you can achieve the objective with your current abilities and resources.
- Relevant: Make sure the goal is important to you and fits in with your larger goals. A meaningful and relevant objective inspires you to keep going. A goal may not be the best fit if it

conflicts with your long-term ambitions or ideals.
- Time-bound: Establishing a deadline instills a sense of urgency and promotes steady advancement. Having a deadline, like "finish a project by the end of the month," helps keep things focused and moving forward.

Methods of Prioritization

Prioritizing your goals is just as important as setting them, and both are necessary for efficient planning. Knowing which chores to prioritize is crucial when there are several competing for your attention. Here are a few popular techniques for setting priorities to keep you on course:

- Eisenhower Matrix: This technique splits work into four sections according to its significance and urgency. There are significant and urgent chores in Quadrant I that need to be completed right away. Important but non-urgent tasks that call for

preemptive planning are included in Quadrant II. Less important duties that can be assigned or removed are found in Quadrants III and IV.
- ABC Prioritization: This technique gives each task a priority level determined by how important it is. "A" activities are the most important and need to be completed right away, while "B" and "C" chores are less important. This approach frees you from the distractions of less vital chores so you can concentrate on what matters most.
- The MoSCoW method

Which stands for must-have, should-have, could-have, and won't-have, is frequently applied in project management. Sorting jobs according to how important they are to the overall objective aids with task prioritization.

Suggestions for Maintaining Focus

Despite having a prioritizing strategy and well-defined goals, remaining on course might be difficult. The following advice can help you stay focused and make progress toward your objectives:

- Divide Big Objectives Into Smaller Steps: Big ambitions might be intimidating. To make success more attainable, break things down into smaller, more doable steps. You can also rejoice in little victories along the way when you use this strategy.
- Establish Frequent Check-Ins: Make it a habit to evaluate your objectives and monitor your advancement. You can set a weekly, monthly, or any other regularity that suits your needs. Frequent check-ins assist you in maintaining accountability and making necessary corrections.
- Make Use of Visual Aids: You may stay focused on your objectives and be reminded of them by using

visual aids such as vision boards, calendars, or sticky notes. This ongoing encouragement can support motivation retention.
- Remain Adaptable: Although having a strategy is crucial, be ready to modify it as needed. Being flexible enables you to adjust to new situations while maintaining focus on your main objectives.
- Seek support and accountability. Talk to loved ones, coworkers, or friends about your objectives so they can encourage you and hold you responsible. It can be helpful to have someone to check in with for extra inspiration and support.
- Acknowledge and Celebrate Your Success: No matter how tiny, acknowledge and celebrate your accomplishments. This encouraging feedback keeps you on track and inspires you to keep pursuing your objectives.

By using these strategies in your planning, you'll be able to prioritize your goals wisely, create realistic goals, and stick to your schedule.

Chapter 5: Getting Past Planning Obstacles: Managing Uncertainty with Resilience

Making plans is not without its difficulties. Plans that have been meticulously formulated might be derailed by stress, uncertainty, and unforeseen circumstances. In this installment of "Planning," we go into methods for surmounting these obstacles, emphasizing the significance of flexibility and adaptability, handling ambiguity, and controlling stress and anxiety. To learn how to handle the challenges of planning with resilience, let's delve into each subject.

Handling Uncertainty

Life and planning are inherently filled with uncertainty. Even if we are unable to anticipate the future with absolute certainty, we can learn coping mechanisms to handle ambiguity and make wise judgments in spite of the unknown. The following strategies can help you cope with uncertainty:

- **Planning for Scenarios**: Take into account a number of potential outcomes and create plans for each, rather than attempting to forecast just one. With this technique, you can adjust your plan as conditions change and be ready for a variety of scenarios.

- **Determine possible hazards:** Identify possible hazards, their likelihood, and how they might affect your plans by doing a risk analysis. Create backup strategies to reduce the impact of these risks and their possible outcomes.
- **Preserve Flexibility:** adopt an attitude of adaptability and receptivity to change. Be prepared to modify your plans if new information becomes available or the situation changes.
- **Concentrate on the Things That You Can Affect**: Even if there may be a lot of things beyond your control, concentrate on the things that you can affect. Focus your efforts on things that you can control and complete.

Controlling anxiety and stress

Planning can be difficult, particularly when there are

competing priorities, short deadlines, or unforeseen setbacks. Sustaining attention and productivity requires effective management of stress and anxiety. Here are a few strategies for reducing stress:

- **Mindfulness and Meditation**: To lower stress and encourage relaxation, try mindfulness exercises like yoga, meditation, or deep breathing. You may approach planning with clarity when you engage in these techniques, which help to build a sense of calm and clarity.
- **Time management**: Being able to manage your time well will make you feel less stressed and overwhelmed. Prioritize your workload, divide things down into smaller, more manageable steps, and plan regular pauses to rest.
- **Seek Support**: When feeling overwhelmed,

don't be afraid to ask friends, family, or coworkers for help. Speaking with someone can help you see things from their point of view and generate ideas for solving problems.
- **Healthy Lifestyle Practices:** Make sleep, food, and exercise your top priorities to maintain a healthy lifestyle. A healthy diet and regular exercise can help lower stress levels and enhance general wellbeing, and getting enough sleep is crucial for clear thinking and sound decision-making.

Adaptability and Flexibility

Successful planning requires flexibility and adaptability in the fast-paced world of today. Plans seldom go exactly as planned, so flexibility in the face of unforeseen events is essential. Here's how to foster adaptation and flexibility:

- **Accept Change:** Accept change as a chance for development and innovation rather than fighting it. Consider obstacles as opportunities for growth and remain receptive to fresh viewpoints.
- **Planning should be done iteratively,** with plans being evaluated and modified on a regular basis in response to input and fresh data. This flexible way of thinking enables quick adjustments to shifting circumstances.
- **Learn from your mistakes:** Making mistakes is a normal aspect of planning. Consider it an opportunity to grow and learn rather than a setback. Determine what went wrong, draw lessons from it, and incorporate those lessons into your next planning endeavors.
- **Keep Your Positive Attitude:** Try not to let

your negative thoughts consume you; instead, concentrate on finding answers. Remain resilient and positive in the face of difficulties, remembering that there are always opportunities for improvement and that setbacks are only temporary. You can overcome planning obstacles and move confidently and resiliently toward success by creating techniques for handling uncertainty, controlling stress and anxiety, and embracing flexibility and adaptability.

Chapter 6: Case Studies for Effective Planning: Gaining Knowledge from Actual Cases

Theory is one thing in the world of planning, but observing the practical application of planning concepts can yield priceless insights. In this part of "planning," we look at case studies that show effective planning in a variety of situations, such as crisis planning, professional project management, and personal planning. By examining these instances, we can learn more about how successful planning techniques result in observable outcomes.

Individual Scheduling: A Day in the Life

Creating a life that is in line with your beliefs, objectives, and priorities is the essence of personal planning, which goes beyond simply managing duties. Let's look at a typical day in the life of Sarah, a busy professional who manages her family, career, and personal objectives:

Sarah's Daily Schedule:

- 6:00 AM: Sarah gets up and begins her day with a regimen that includes working out, meditating, and making a nutritious breakfast.
- 7:00 AM: She goes over her day agenda, setting priorities and allotting time for crucial events.

Work-Life Harmony:

- 9:00 AM: Sarah utilizes time management strategies at work to

maintain concentration and productivity. She schedules dedicated time slots for in-depth work, meetings, and relaxation.
- 6:00 PM: Sarah enjoys spending time with her family, having supper together, and doing recreational activities after work.

Setting and reflecting on goals:

- 8:00 PM: Sarah evaluates her day and makes plans for the following one in the evening. Based on her progress, she modifies her goals and pinpoints areas in need of improvement.

Sarah's method of personal planning highlights the value of prioritizing tasks, using time wisely, and striking a balance between personal and professional life.

Project management in professional planning

In the business world, meeting deadlines and financial constraints requires efficient project management. Let's look at a real-world instance of a project managed successfully:
Case Study: Introducing a New Item

- **Objective:** The objective is to introduce a new product line and gain a sizable market share in less than six months.
- **Phase of planning:** The project manager determines target demographics, carries out in-depth market research, and establishes clear launch goals.
- **Resource Allocation:** After the project team is put together, each member is given a defined set of duties. Distribution,

marketing, and product creation all have budgets.
- **Timeline Creation:** A thorough schedule is made, highlighting significant dates and completion dates for every stage of the undertaking.
- **Risk management**: This involves identifying and proactively addressing potential hazards through contingency plans, such as supply chain disruptions or competitor actions.
- **Execution**: The project team collaborates to carry out the plan, periodically assessing its progress and making necessary adjustments to its tactics.
- **Launch and Assessment:** Sales of the new product surpass projections after a successful launch. The project team carries out a comprehensive review following launch in order to pinpoint areas that require improvement and lessons learned.

In order to successfully complete a project, this case study emphasizes the significance of strategic planning, efficient resource allocation, and proactive risk management.

Crisis Management Planning: Actual Case Studies

During catastrophic events like natural catastrophes or worldwide pandemics, having a well-thought-out plan can make the difference between chaos and resilience. Let's look at two actual instances of crisis planning:

Case Study 1: Being Ready for Disasters

- **Aim:** Minimizing the effects of a natural disaster on a community is the aim.
- **Planning**: Local governments create thorough plans for disaster preparedness that include escape routes, emergency

shelters, and communication guidelines.
- **Training and Simulation:** To guarantee preparedness and coordination in the case of a disaster, emergency personnel participate in frequent training exercises and simulations.
- **Engagement with the Community:** Information regarding emergency supplies, evacuation routes, and communication systems is disseminated across the community in advance of a crisis.
- **Response and Recovery:** Emergency responders move swiftly to coordinate relief activities and put the preparedness plan into action when a disaster strikes. During the healing process, the community joins together to help one another.

Case Study No. 2: Reaction to the Pandemic

- **Objective:** Protecting public health and preventing the spread of a worldwide pandemic are the main objectives.
- **Public Health Measures:** To stop the illness from spreading, governments enforce public health measures, including mask laws, social separation, and vaccine drives.
- **Healthcare Preparedness:** By building more space, obtaining necessary supplies, and putting infection control procedures in place, hospitals and other healthcare facilities get ready for a surge of patients.
- **Economic Support:** In order to help people and businesses affected by the pandemic, governments offer financial aid, unemployment insurance, and small business loans.

- **Research and Innovation:** To tackle the virus, scientists and researchers are working nonstop to produce vaccines, therapies, and diagnostic tests.

These case studies highlight how important preparation is to crisis management, covering readiness, reaction, and rehabilitation activities.

We may learn important lessons from these real-world instances of effective planning and apply them to our own planning initiatives, whether they be for personal, career, or emergency situations. Having a plan is not enough to make effective planning; you also need to be ready for anything unexpected and able to adjust and bounce back quickly.

Chapter 7: Planning's Future: Managing Change in a Changing World

The dynamic field of planning is always impacted by new developments in technology, changes in society, and fashion trends. In this installment of "Planning," we delve into the future of planning, emphasizing new developments, the influence of technology, and the shifting function of planning in a world that is changing quickly. Let's look at how planning is predicted to change and what those implications are for people and businesses.

Planning Trends

A multitude of trends reflecting shifts in technology, society, and the environment will influence planning in the future. The following major developments will have an effect on planning practices in the upcoming years:

- **Distant Work and Virtual Collaboration:** The emergence of tools for virtual collaboration and distant work has revolutionized how we communicate and organize. Planning tools must change to accommodate virtual teams and dispersed work environments as more people contribute remotely or work from home.
- **Sustainability and Green Initiatives:** Planning will place a greater emphasis on sustainability and green initiatives as environmental concerns gain traction. This movement emphasizes lowering carbon footprints and fostering eco-friendly behaviors, and it has an impact on company

practices, urban development, and individual lifestyles.

- **Inclusive Planning:** Diversity and inclusivity are increasingly important components of planning procedures. Planning that is inclusive ensures that a range of perspectives are heard and included, resulting in more equitable and thorough plans. Workplace procedures, community involvement, and urban development are all impacted by this tendency.
- **Planning that is Flexible and Agile:** Planning that is Flexible and Agile is becoming more and more necessary. Originally created for software development, agile approaches are now being used in various industries, with an emphasis on iterative planning and flexibility in response to changing circumstances.

How Technology Affects Planning

The future of planning is significantly shaped by technology. The planning industry is changing quickly due to the development of digital technologies, automation, and artificial intelligence (AI). Here are some ways that technology is affecting planning:

- **Digital Planning Tools:** Project management, time management, and collaborative planning software are getting more and more advanced. Advanced capabilities for work tracking, resource allocation, and team collaboration are available in tools like Trello, Asana, and Microsoft Project.
- **Automation and artificial intelligence (AI):** These two technologies are optimizing planning procedures. Planners may

concentrate on higher-level decision-making by using automation technologies to handle monotonous chores, while AI-driven analytics can evaluate massive volumes of data to find trends and make forecasts.
- **Data-Driven Planning:** Data-driven planning is made possible by the availability of huge data and sophisticated analytics. Planners are able to use data to track important indicators, evaluate trends, and make well-informed decisions. This data-driven strategy lowers uncertainty and increases accuracy.
- **Virtual reality (VR) and augmented reality (AR)** are two emerging technologies that are being used in planning, particularly in architecture and urban planning. With the aid of these tools, planners can see projects in a virtual setting, giving

them a realistic perspective on suggested modifications and promoting improved decision-making.

Planning's Function in a Changing World

Planning's function is to alter to keep up with the needs of a world that is changing quickly. Planning needs to change to stay current and useful as societal, environmental, and technological developments pick up speed. The predicted evolution of planning's role is as follows:

- **Resilience and adaptability:** Planning must place a high priority on resilience and adaptability while dealing with ambiguity. In an uncertain environment, being able to modify plans and react to unforeseen events is essential for success.

- **Cross-Disciplinary Collaboration:** Experts from different disciplines are working together more and more in planning. A greater variety of requirements and viewpoints are addressed in more comprehensive plans created using this cross-disciplinary approach, which also encourages creativity.
- **Social Influence:** Planning is becoming more concerned with the social influence and well-being of the community. In order to promote inclusive and equitable outcomes, planners take society's impact into account while making decisions.
- **Global Perspective:** As globalization and climate change demand international cooperation, planning is becoming more global in scope. Planners have to think about the bigger picture

while making decisions and strive to find solutions that will benefit everyone on the planet.

Through comprehension of these patterns, innovations in technology, and the changing function of planning, people and institutions can more adeptly maneuver through the future. A combination of conventional methods and cutting-edge technologies will be needed for effective planning, with a focus on social impact, inclusion, and adaptability. Planners will be essential in shaping a future that is more equal and sustainable as the globe changes.

Conclusion and Next Moves: Equipping You for Success in Future Planning

As we draw to a close our exploration of "planning," it is important to consider the major ideas we have covered, suggest resources for additional education, and encourage you to continue being successful in your planning. Let's review the main points, offer further resources for those who are keen to learn more, and encourage you to keep using efficient planning techniques in your personal and professional lives.

An overview of the main ideas

We have studied the foundational ideas of planning in this book, including subjects like goal-setting, time management, risk assessment, and flexibility. Below is a synopsis of the main ideas we've discussed:

- **Setting smart goals:** This is essential to good planning. Clear, measurable, attainable, relevant and time-bound goals are what they should be..
- **Time management:** Effective time management, work prioritization, and distraction reduction are critical abilities for effective planning.
- **Risk management:** Three essential elements of good planning are recognizing possible hazards, creating backup plans, and remaining adaptable.
- **Adaptability:** The success of planning depends on one's capacity to accept ambiguity, change course when necessary, and adapt to changing conditions. Technology: Planning efficacy and efficiency can

be increased by utilizing digital tools, automation, and data-driven insights.
- **Inclusivity:** Taking into account many viewpoints, including stakeholders, and encouraging fairness and accessibility in the decision-making process are all components of inclusive planning.

Sources for Additional Education

Numerous materials are available for people who are keen to gain a deeper understanding of planning ideas and processes. The following lists of suggested reads, classes, and websites to check out:

- **Novels:**

  - Money planner: managing your money by Israel Daniel.

- **Time Classes:**

    - LinkedIn Learning's Time Management Fundamentals course
    - Coursera's "Project Management Basics"
    - "Udemy's "Agile for Everyone"

- **Web sites:**

    - The Harvard Business Review provides case studies and articles on a range of planning and management-related topics. Project
    - Management Institute (PMI): offers webinars, certifications, and resources to project managers.
    - TED Talks: Contains

motivational speeches on subjects including creativity, time management, and goal-setting.

Motivation for Ongoing Planning Achievement

Recall that planning and goal-achieving are journeys, not destinations, as you proceed on your path to success. Here are some inspirational quotes to keep you motivated along the way:

- **Remain Concentrated**: Remain focused on your priorities and keep your goals in sight. Setbacks and distractions are unavoidable, but overcoming them requires persistence.
- **Celebrate Your Progress:** Honor all of your accomplishments, no matter how modest. Every step you take toward your objectives is worthwhile

and should be acknowledged.
- **Learn from Setbacks:** View failure as a chance for development and education. Consider what went wrong in the past, adjust your approach and continue nevertheless.
- **Seek Assistance:** Don't be afraid to ask friends, family, or mentors for assistance. Embrace the company of positive and inspiring individuals in your life.
- **Remain Adaptable:** Show that you are prepared to change courses as necessary. Although life is unpredictable, your capacity for adaptation guarantees that you will be able to face obstacles head-on.
- **Continue Learning:** Never give up on acquiring new information. As the world is always changing, it will be beneficial to you to

remain inquisitive and flexible while you plan.

Recall that the planning process involves more than just getting where you're going; it's also about the development and transformation you go through on the route. You may attain your objectives and design the life you want by putting the concepts and methods in this book to use together with a resilient and persistent mentality. Cheers to your ongoing success with planning!

www.ingramcontent.com/pod-product-compliance
Lightning Source LLC
Chambersburg PA
CBHW070416230526
45471CB00006B/2834